R6O

INSIGHT

six south african poets

Nosipho Kota

Alex Mboshwa Mohlabeng

Myesha Jenkins

Ayanda Billie

Themba Ka Mathe

Righteous the Common Man

Edited by

Alan Finaly
&
Siphiwe Ka Ngwenya

First published in 2003 by
TIMBILA Poetry Project
41 Hans van Rensburg Street
Rampie Smit Building
Suite E
Polokwane 0700

AND

BILA Publishers & Communications
PO Box 470
Elim Hospital
0960 Limpopo Province
Republic of South Africa

INSIGHT
© Contributors

ISBN: 0-620-29428-0

The publisher acknowledges financial assistance for the
publication of this work from INTERFUND and the
National Development Agency.

INTERFUND

Cover Design & Layout:
Jo Nhlapo

Contents

Introduction

i. Nosipho Kota
(BARE SOUL)

ii. Alex Mohlabeng
(WE WEEP NOT)

iii. Myesha Jenkins
(BREAKING THE SURFACE)

iv. Ayanda Billie
(FORBIDDEN TO DREAM)

v. Themba ka Mathe
(DISTURBING THE DEAD)

vi. Righteous The Common Man
(THE SEED OF LIFE)

Introduction

This collection of new poetry was work-shopped in Polokwane and Johannesburg – it is the result of the hard work by the Timbila Poetry Project and writers who have gathered spontaneously under the Timbila umbrella. It is designed to give them a voice and place in the publishing arena – a sounding.

This book has been a collaboration. The editors – who acted more as facilitators – worked individually with the poets, then as part of the group, talking about how the book should look and feel. Poets were encouraged to make their own selections, to say what they needed to say.

Words that seem important to describe undercurrents in this poetry are: endurance, defeat, resolution, hunger, gentleness, desire and defiance – broad enough to encompass a whole panorama of living emotions, but which take on particular resonances in the South African context.

For instance, the emotional annihilation that is the shadow of "the tiny zinc-capped hovel [that] stands like a dumped tin writ large" or the shebeen where bodies "strewed the slummy yard/ Likepatients in a hospital hall". It's the place "clouded by pain" where "like a cage bird in my cell/ I watch the world pass me by".

There are absences (notably of the father) and moments of terrible defeat"

Yes, they said
Keep on trying
Dark child
Until you die
It will be over someday

The victories in this poetry are the flashes of resolution, defiance – sexual and political...

Remember me the common man
from the land of the common people
where poverty pierces souls of the feeble
like needles do skins of dizzy crack junkies

or

To want to be
        A relentless killer woman
        A militant organising mother woman
        An earth strong rooted woman
        An intelligent courageous leader woman
A blood witch warrior woman
An unassuming worker-bee spy woman
No one will encourage that

and the places of gentleness and desire, even while acknowledg-
ing absence:

I wish I could be like dust,
rush out with the wind,
as it hisses to the mountains…

I wish I can take a ride,
with the stars that shine no more at daytime,
but come out at night to challenge the sky.

These are new poets, working in new directions, some of them
only at the beginning of their voices. There is at times a healthy
experimentation with language, and a bold new treatment and
exploration of ideas – a desire, ultimately, for insight, while look-
ing out: in sight. Read it and hear where they want to go…

Alan Finlay and Siphiwe Ka Ngwenya
Editors

Nosipho Kota

Bare Soul

LOOKING FOR GOD

Through every heartache
i looked for you
through every birth
i searched for you
in the eyes of toddlers
playing in gap-taps
in the weary steps of old men
i looked for you
in street corners
i looked for you
in the betrayal of friends
in the mockery of enemies
in the words uttered by satisfied lovers,
i looked for you
in the poems that I write
i looked for your intervention
in the letters
i scribbled to lost lovers
in the songs
that I composes at dawn
i was looking for you,
i was looking for God.

BARE SOUL

You have big brown eyes
that touched my inner being
revealing my bare soul.

You have a lovely smile
that made me stare into your eyes
and hold the memory of it forever.

YOUR SOFT BELLY

I like my body more,
when it is with your body.
I like how it feel like,
underneath yours.
Your soft belly touching mine,
your arms holding me,
its strength awesome.
I like my body,
when it joins with yours,
for the emotions it evokes in me,
daring ones,
triumphant ones

WHEN YOU DIED

the landscape changed
the coffee that I was drinking turned cold,
the bath-water in my basin turned cold,
the dogs stopped barking
the chicken came home
the children's giggles vanished
when you died

TRUTH

The stench of truth
like the smell of flesh burning,
eats away
bit by bit,
at all the memories,
of that time, I spent with you.

Because when I am with you,
I can smell the rain,
the richness of the soil,
feels me up.
like you do.

TOWNSHIP WOMAN

There is a woman in our township
She lived by herself in a two-bedroomed
house
Her cats are her only children
there are huge trees around her yard.

She is called igqwirha
because she is dark-skinned,
old and wrinkled.
She wears black attire and that qualifies her
as a witch.

There is a woman in our township
she lives alone,
her husband died.
Her children are gone.

She is called umhlolokazi.
The dogs bark at her.
Taxi drivers don't want her in their taxis,
its assumed she'll bring bad luck.

There is a woman in our township
she lives alone,
in her subsidised house.

She is called amarosha,
by other woman,
who thinks that she is out to get their men.
no one invites her to the social gatherings.

There is a woman in our township
She is an alcoholic
She drinks herself to oblivion.

She is called unotap,
she uses her children's maintenance grant
to fund her booze consumption.

There is a woman in our township
She is baby –making machine
She produces a child every two years.

She is called inkomazi
She seldom goes out,
cause she has to breastfeed her lot.

There is a woman in our township
She is a small business woman,
And asks nothing from nobody.

She is called Iscwinana
Her home is well-furnished.
She eats out in fancy restaurants.

There is a woman in our township.
She shops at exclusive boutiques,
her wallet is bulging with credit cards.

She is called umadam.
Her hobbies include going to the movies,
and come Sunday morning, she's off to
Health and Racquet.

There is a woman in our township.
She is unemployed.
She basks in the sun all day long, gossiping.

She is called unolokishi.
She is obsessed with other people's affairs,

drinking tea with our people's miseries.

There is a woman in our township
She is beggar and thief.
She's ungrateful

She is called ubergie,
She takes without permission.
And would sell her soul for a piece of meat.

There a woman in our township
She is a beggar and thief.
She's ungrateful.

She's called ubergie,
she takes without permission.
And would sell her soul for a piece of meat.

There is a woman in our township
she is a shebeen queen.
Men's wages are her means of survival.

She is called unosekeni.
She is lod and speaks non-stop.
She should have become a soccer-commen-
tator.

There is a woman in our township
She sells vegetables at the bus terminal.
She earns her living doing laundry for Mrs
van Niekerk.

She is called unokhitshi.
She wears takkies and blue overalls, with a
pretty apron,
that madam gave her for Christmas.

There is a woman in our township.
She is happily married or so she says.
She eats Kentucky Fried Chicken every
Friday.

She is called umastandi.
She looks after children and her in-laws.
Does her chores to perfection,
on month-ends her husband's wages is
tucked in her bosom.

THE SWINGING DOORS

The heart of a woman
bottles up stores of mercy
piled in cane baskets
safely tucked away
In it there are yesterday's moans,
today's expectations and
tomorrow's wishes.

MY WISH

I wish I could be like dust
rush out with the wind,
as it hisses to the mountains.

I wish I could move with the restless sea,
to its seascapes,
to see where sea creatures live.

I wish I could hide with the moon,
to see where the other pieces hide,
and see them take shape when the moon is full.

I wish I can take a ride,
with the stars that shine no more at daytime,
but come out at night to challenge the sky.

LIKE A LOG

My body
is mine,
skin ,
blood and veins.

When you enter,
you push,
you thrust,
and fumble in.

It eludes me,
how you groan and moan,
sweat and sigh,
while I lay there,
revolted.

HE SENT ME FLOWERS TODAY

He sent me flowers today
he didn't have to,
but he did it anyway.

They were beautiful flowers,
don't know what they are called,
but he sent me flowers today.

He sent the flowers,
through a messenger,
who eagerly waited on my door for a tip.

He sent me
love-scented flowers,
and at every one smell of flower, I remem-
bered his face.

He sent me flowers,
but because he has never sent me flowers
before,
I new something was wrong.

He sent me flowers,
because in his own way,
he was telling me that which he could not
articulate in words.

He sent me flowers,
to say he was sorry,
let us let bygones be bygones.

AUTOBIOGRAPHY

I was born in 1974
In the last few years, I have not been to my
birth-place.

At ten I was homeless
At eleven and a half, I started menstruating
no one celebrated my girlhood.

Some people know all about plants and fish
I know separation.

Some people can recite all about the stars
I recite absences.
They have been my blanket for as long as I
can recall.

I have spent a night in jail
for something that I didn't do,
I have slept in exotic hotels,
it felt good to sleep in clean, white cotton
sheets,
in a cold weather, sheltered from its claws.

At twenty-one
no one threw a party,
for reaching adulthood safe.
At twenty-two
I flew to Denmark
for sixteen straight hours.

I drank, smoked ganja but not everyday.
They tried to tear me away from the Danish
beer,
it didn't work.
I earned my living

through my humble but remarkable writings.

I have deceived most men in my life,
because they deserved it,
I never talked behind my friend's back,
unless it was absolutely necessary.

I have lied in the past, so as not to hurt people,
But I have also lied for no reason at all.

In 1992, I lost my father
cried bitter tears of unfinished business.

Cancer has not caught up with me yet,
but my real worry is HIV/AIDS.
I will never be a president like Thabo
but would surely love to be an MP,
sit on my butt all day long,
ride in the famous gravy train.

In shortly, my friends
even if things are not looking up for me today,
I can safely say,
that I have lived like a human being.

A HOUSE

There have been days
when I have felt
like a house
left
destitute
on a mountain-top

IN YOU

In you,
I have seen the footprints
of my soul,
woven,
in tiny little threads of wool.
I have seen my dreams,
lurking.

FOR KAITLIN

Your eyes are like the deep-end
of the ocean
suave and dazzling.
Your eyelashes like a river
beneath a river.
Your voice like that of
whales calling at dawn.

ON HIS FUNERAL

His obituary
Was brief and short.

Only twelve lines.

He left no grieving spouse.
No children, no parents.

His coffin lay on the concrete stoep,
Plain cheap wood.

No flowers
No tears

No speeches
No lies

Just a simple funeral of a young man.

IN

Alex
Mohlabeng

We Weep Not

WE WEEP NOT

We weep not
When the souls of sages
Are rested,
Through the furrowed faces
Of their bleary-eyed kin
Sob stridently
Pining for their grey-haired,
The wrinkles-riddled loved ones.

We weep not
When we plant them
In underground charnel houses.
Earth takes them back,
As we sing solemn threnodies
And recite written elegies.
Thus we elevate their fallen spirits
To the land of ancestors
Where they fill void seats
That awaits their presence.

We weep not
When the souls of sages
Are laid to rest.
Their kin we apprise:
As we revere their spirits,
They shall watch over us,
Give us abundant guidance
For their pails are overflowing
With wisdom.
They will refuse to die
And live in absolute oblivion.

THE HUNTER

Journeying homewards,
The sweltering hunter
Came clutching a knobkierie
Carrying a gory sack
Riddled with a buzz.

Caught slumbering in its hole
This rabbit was clobbered, dead.

With feet starting to slack,
His greedy eyes caught
The sight of lame game
Limping across the golden savanna.
Just wandering.

His heart purred, excitement.
"My hungry family back home
Will hunger no more"

Impetuously,
He relinquished the sack.
Pursued the injured antelope.
It strained its sinews
And hopped away,
Leaving him sweat-drenched
And panting under the simmering sun.

Then he terribly mourned
For both his escaped quarry
And the abandoned sack he found,
Vanished into thing air.

SHEBEEN INVENTION

From that house there
A man came out,
Staggering,
With a crooked chameleon gait,
His pants wetted, unabashed,
Going to his wife and kids.

Leaving behind him,
A cacophony of noises;
Cracking raucous laughter,
Raging fights,
Clanging of steel mugs
And drunken wagging tongues.

They daily trudge from town
For their mugful of concoction
Illicitly brewed
By the law flouting
Backyard brewer.

They strewed the slummy yard
Like patients in a hospital hall.
Sat on wooden benches,
Sprawled in drunken stupor
On the dampened ground
Of smelly urine and liquor,
Mumbled madly in a daze
Like madmen,
Riddled with purulent black pimples;
Peeled pink skin; red lips;
Trembling;
Walking an awkward gait

The shebeen invention at work.
'Killer',
'Quick kicker'.
Names by which it is known
By the township folk.

IF I HAVE TO SING

If I have to sing,
I shall chant loud a tune
To muffle the maddening din
Of rifles in stricken streets
And seal delicate ears
Of babies in bared houses
Impaled by shots stings

I shall chorus with a choir
To cover for warmth,
With summer's large plumage,
Waifs in winter's cold nights
Squirming in pockets of cities,
Behind those tall buildings
Standing like high hills
That shed shades to one another.

I shall sing them lullabies
And rock them to rest
In cradles of foul floors.
They will have dreams of wealth
And their rags shall be
Swish coverings of gossamer silk
In the comfort of mind mansions.

If I have to sing,
I shall sing a song
To soothe battered bodies
Of women,
Of children
Screeching in their homes,
Behind the shadows.
Their wails imploring for mercy.

I shall sing a lasting slogan
To lift the burdens on heads
Of mothers bearing babies
On their sore backs,
On their way to nowhere
And place tents of refuge
For their fleeing forms.

For those pining for peace,
I shall sing a sacred hymn
To summon doves from their dwellings
To hover above in a host
And pervade shreds of serenity
On all the stricken places.

If I have to sing,
I shall plead in prayer song
For those with empty stomachs
Foraging for food in bins,
With the same great GOD
Who rained manna
In the desert of death.

If I have to sing,
I shall vomit out my voice
And sing a solo in fortissimo
To cause a great change,
If only my songs
Could be the elixir of lives.

THE FIELD WORKER'S LAMENT

By congealed blisters
On these rough palms
Young baas became pretty plump
And big-bellied
Before my own old eyes
Surfeiting in his villa
The progeny of the soil
That is me.

This dark loam land,
Inside whose bowels
My soul lies sown,
I've cradled with care
Like a mother would her own.
Tended and toiled and nurtured,
Dirt drenched,
That my own
May live more abundantly.

And from the broiler
Of my blackened body
Baked daily by the heat,
My sweat watered this soil
The soil strewn with crops
In the growing greenery.

And like a still rock
I withstood all odds,
For him,
For his fathers before
This fledgling,

That has just flapped wings,
To rid of a senile being,
I shall cast with a curse
Fierce and fatal.
Thus I speak my heart.
This pain I can't smolder
And be a sullen self.

OLD MEN

Once they sat on wooden stools
And arched around
Sorghum beer filled gourds
They began to regale us-
Enchanted-
With bloodcurdling tales of woe
Leaving us gazing and gawping
With amazement.
And the amusing tales of adventure
As they relived past years.

Everytime they merrily relish
Under the marula tree,
Calabashesful of sorghum beer
Brewed by old village women
With great care,
We long for tales time:
The pounding of fearful hearts
And the tickling of tummies.

SHARK

Fierce and bloodlust-eyed
Is the toperdo-like shark,
Majestic in his movements.
This monomanic with a mission:
To savage mercilessly to death
With jagged razor-sharp teeth,
Prey he swiftly swims to hunt,
Sleeplessly at the sea depths.
His hunger is never assuaged.

I saw my black brothers
Who are devoured by devilish minds
And like foolish escapades,
Parody ways of this monster:
Lilting down the dusty streets
Of my sordid township
In the dead of night
Brandishing blades
That luminate in the dark
To wait in the street corners
And badly lacerate bodies
Of victims whose blood they binge,
Unquenched.

ENRAGED HEAVENS

Enraged heavens
Let loose their ferocious rage
On the scurvy world.

To signal a siege
To the earth
The shaded skies
Brandished jagged blades
Amid the distant rumble
That shook like a quake.

Suffocate by chemical fumes
Billowing from gigantic factory chimneys
And the charred car exhausts
That spew like giant cigarettes,
Heavy clouds shed tears-
Anger flaring-up-
Preceded by the sinister squall
Pelting acid rain in pellets
Plaguing the vegetation fields
That feed us.

FIRST DAY AT SCHOOL

I was a little bumpkin
In oversized khakhi shorts and shirt
Clutching pencil and slate.
Bare feet
The sun was out.
I needed some pluck-
The runt from the country-
To avert the brawny bullies
Who jolted and hustled us;
The grassy school yard strewn
With elated faces,
Stone faces,
Faces with woeful intentions
Uniformed
Like busy bodies of termites.

I was awed:
Grown ups mounting the dais
When the bell clanged
Summoning us to converge;
Long rows of lesson rooms
Standing like coal train carriages
At Pietersburg station.

The whole spectacle conjured up
The ugly indelible memory:
My brother; the cane;
Weals on his black buttocks,
Grimacing,
As he told the tale.
Apprehension took hold.
And then I remembered
That from then on,
He began to loathe school.

A SAGE

I am a citrus tree
In its dotage
Pregnant with succulent fruit
That never shrivel and drop
Under the scorching sun.
Fruit not fatal if surfeited,
Sagging the leafy arms
Waiting to be picked by passers-by
And squeezed of all juiced
Of the sage brains I possess.
The hard life I endured
And the fruits thereof I relished.

A MARKET BOY

His satchel rested.
The day's lesson was done.
The burning blue skies
Parched his young lips,
Pale from hunger.
In his tiny tummy,
Growled some strange beast.

A big bowl-
Full of mounds of huge greens-
Mounted his heavy head.
He stood on bare-feet,
Legs weary and weak,
To tread on dusty streets
And market the hip.

With a bored pair of pupils,
Gazed at the playgrouds
Thronged with cheerful children
Frisking in great frolic fun
As if intending to scorn him.

He left lonely and desolate
And began to slowly slack
As if queer
Like a poor prospector
Amid the sea of sand.
His lone heart lamented:
"Will I forever be denied
The pleasure of play?"

WOMEN NEIGHBOURS

The strident skirmish
Of sordid women neighbours–
One face daubed with mud musk–
Halted the morning stillness.
Foul imprecations were flung
Over the sagging wire fence
Arms akimbo
Amid frenetic gesticulations–
Fore-fingers poking the air
In profound virulent rage.

The dew-drenched feet,
Sleep curtained eyes of children
Converged on
To watch the spectacle–
A common sight to them–
Muttered. Chuckled.
Quacked with laughter, amused.

And as the battle thawed,
Returned home aping
With their lissom limps,
As if they've just been
To a big screen movie,
The erratic actions,
The baring of thighs and arms
By their sordid mothers,
And living the hate
That comes with them.

THE SHACK

The debilitating spectre of hunger
We endure
Invokes no mercy
In the wealthy callous people
Of my land

Summer.
Hot like clay hardening kiln
The tiny zinc-capped hovel
With a pungent odour
In which we are compressed;
Mother,
My squalid siblings and I,
Stands like a dumped tin writ large.
Crammed.
Things hanging, piling, stuffed,
Floating on the floor.

The rusty door hinges
Daily creaks a sombre song-
The melancholic blues in us.
Little gullies stagnant
Like moat around a castle,
Carry ravaging water-borne ills.

Winter.
A pall of smoke
Churning from the burning brazier
And the tyre bonfire
Stuffing our sick lungs.
And we shudder

In our oblong shining igloo
Sounding the song of clattering teeth.
The debilitating spectre of hunger
We endure invokes no mercy
In the wealthy callous people
Of my land.

THE AFRICAN SUN

All was well.
The African sun blazing
over all beings.
Stately hanging
high on the azure sky.
Wearing a buoyant face
as if to amuse us.
Her face,
the semblance of a heart.

Beneath her,
village girls come walking
through the winding narrow way
like a large snake sliding
on the low-lying grass.
Semi-stark and their feet
bared. Fashioned with
shimmering peals and beads.
Gourds of river water
and bunches of branches
perching on their heads.

Gathered in an arch
in the court yard,
men, minds strained to disentangle
puzzles of their land.
They drink from calabashes,
home-brewed beer,
their pride.

Women with rheumy eyes
smothered in a reek of faggots
like a clouds clustered plane,
to prepare good victuals
in hot old scruffy claypots.

Generations are fed of them.

Kid shepherds
tend the bleating sheep,
herds of horned cattle
and goats, their heirlooms,
on the green grounds
pregnant with nurturing loam.

They revered as royalty,
spirits of their distant dead
in a wealthy world
of milk and honeyed homes.

Until from the west
verminous hosts came
under the scarlet sky
in a silhouette
like a plague of locusts
sinister in its swaying swam,
clutching black books
covered in cassocks
rosaries dangling on chests;
amulets with which
to avert evil.

Their faces contorted in grin
with teeth white as snow
to mar and cleave a core
of a people and its lore,
derelict with no relics.
Then we mourn the glare
of the African sun that sets
on its fret, bemoaning.

Myesha
Jenkins

Breaking the Surface

NATAL

Green ocean
waves shimmer
across the hills
in the breeze
as far
as I can see
awash in sweat
drenched from salt tears
crashing on abundant land
stained with the blood
of those who now
harvest our
sweetness
sugar cane
of Natal.

POSSESSION

We dance for God
And jump and shout and flail and weep.

Bodies open to power from this universe
sway and sweat possessed with energy
unknown

From the dust of our rhythmic feet
the spirit rises from the earth

Singing praises to the heavens
to call down the soul's peace

Entering one and many
to teach the way, open the path, warn of the
dangers

Heartbeats drum to clapping staccato hands
and the words of God envelope all meaning.

EXHALT HIM

The albino boy
in the sea of blackness
gazed at Selif Keita

When the crowd began to sway
the albino boy
sang with Selif Keita

But at the end
up front, on the stage
the albino boy
danced with Selif Keita.

Ascension.

GIRLFRIENDS

I love my girlfriends
they lift me up

Its good to have
someone
who cares
enough
to always
listen

The job
that man
this body

Sharing
Remembering
Dreaming

I love my girlfriends

UNCERTAINTY

In my mind
I want to run in the fields
roll in the grass
twine in your legs
stroke your back
tickle your sides
All the things that lovers do

But I sit in my room
choked by uncertainty
and knawing doubts
in my heart.

THE MAGICIAN

What you do is not magic you said
But what is it then
That can reach into my soul
Search out my fears
Then play them back to me in a dance of joy
How did you find your way to my heart
Closed from human warmth for so long
Through this maze of darkness
Wandering into all the back rooms
Even those covered with cobwebs and thick dust
You fling open the doors and windows
In my walled-off spaces
Letting in air and light and finally heat
Only a magician could bring tears from the stone I have become
Only magic can stir such passion from this dry and flattened land-
scape

A shoot of green bursts free

REVOLUTIONARY WOMAN

Don't admire a revolutionary woman
No one will encourage that

To want to be
A relentless killer woman
A militant organising mother woman
An earth strong rooted woman
An intelligent courageous leader woman
A blood witch warrior woman
An unassuming worker-bee spy woman

No one will encourage that
To want to be
A Dora Maria Tellez, Nora Astorga,
Haydee Santamaria kind of woman
An Asata Shakur, Nguyen Thi Binh,
Laila Khaled kind of woman
A Mila Aguilar, Lolita Lebron, Bernadette
Develin
kind of woman
A Marion Sparg, Cheryl Carolus, Thenjiwe
Mthintso
kind of woman

No one will encourage that

Don't admire a revolutionary woman
Praise her
Love her
Dream of her
Sing for her
Honour her
Emulate her

Don't admire a revolutionary woman

SLEEP LOVING

Like starfish
we float in the ocean of unconsciousness
entangled in the protuberances of one
another
we attach with soft suckers
changing forms as we roll around and over
disengage with a muscular contraction
again gliding into another crevice of the
other
lolling tongues know the salt of our waters
past
and we drift in and out
aware even in sleep
comforted by this buoyant tenderness
in the deep intimacy of night.

BAD NEWS FOR MADIBA

As we celebrate
the triumph of your vision
we are changed
not by the righteousness
of new relations
but by the individualism
and greed
of the enemy.

ANIMAL

that animal
that was hiding
comes awake
lives in me
driving
pulsing
sweating
feeling my body
frantic
and nothing else
desperate in its
desire to have you
deeper
harder
grabbing it
wet
pulling it
all over me
inside out of me
pushing it
looking in your eyes
seeing to a new place
when we opened up
it came out
and we both survived
toe to toe
and liked it.

NO QUEENS HERE

No, I am not your queen
that would imply
privilege and sloth
servants and slaves.
How could you think that of me?

And the beauty of a flower
would doom me to
a fleeting glory,
perhaps trampled in a cow field,
while my ripeness continues as mango scent.
Don't you know?

Despite my colouring,
this chocolate ain't always sweet.
No, I hardly bring on
childhood delight. not a precious new toy.
Would you miss my masala/mole/kimchee
complexity and taste?

The paens to motherhood
are exhausting, mythologised
meaningless to my barren womb.
Not all women are mothers,
What do you say to us?

I rail against perfection
reject your rambling fantasies,
despise the dizzy heights of your pedestals,
cringe at your adoration.
Why would you set me so far apart
from you?

No queens, no flowers, no sweeties, no fantasy
mamas.

I am content
to just be
a black woman
compared to nothing else.

LITCHI

Like that litchi you loved so well
I lay brown and a little rough
protecting my precious inner fruit
deceiving all but the most knowing

That first bite
oozes sweetness into your mouth
juice streaming down your chin
biting, stripping, squeezing
the outer cover is removed
revealing flesh
soft, fragrant, fragile
caressing your tongue
and sucking throat
firm, cool, delicate
you enjoy the freshness

Once finished
you roll the seed around in your mouth
till the last of the taste
dissolves into memory.

Then you spit it out.

LOVE MARKS

The imprint of you
tattoos my body
head to toe
inside and out
covers me with your
weight and musky smell.

Peeling layer by layer
I discover
how complete
your penetration has been
marking me with
fresh scars of imperfection.

Stripping off the skin
to rid myself of this betrayal
tearing out the flesh piece by piece
my brain's convolutions ooze reason and
beauty
my heart still dripping bloodtears
out of my belly the stillborn child with
open eyes.

And I continue peeling
clawing at this shadow
deeper than you ever knew
there is still you
criss-crossing the bones
of my back, my thighs, my ankles

Cleansed by fire
the small mound now rests
as ashes of who I once was
lying in black and white
forming your smile

MID LIFE REFLECTIONS

A woman in the middle of life
can stop and be still
moving gently through space
She only runs when something necessary
must be done.

A woman in the middle of life
finds familiar fairies and devils alike
relishing their periodic visits
comfortable in the intimacy
with all.

She has a history
roots sunk deep to many places
like webs in caves of past lives
her memories varied and rich
her few friends trusted and true.

A woman in the middle of life
still enjoys a lusty lover
and savors the taste of his sweat
long after he's gone.

Blooming in roundness
she is shedding skin
and sits in a new body
no longer firm but comfortable.

A woman in the middle of life
looks upward often
in response to the call of the moon
and whisper of raging sunset.

She lives to know more
of fertile seas and ancient songs
blinked from the eye of God
and remains amazed
by the colors of green

MAKING POEMS

I lie when I say
a poem just comes
first there is
a restlessness
vaguely agitated
sometimes sleepless nights
unfocused energy
slipping as my mind loosens
altered by a desire
to submerge into beauty
escape into the subtlety of
a word reality

I feel it coming
slowly
scratching
building
spinning
into words.

I am never sure
what is stirring
what will come out
how it will shape.

I want to take the dive
into the unfathomable
swoop down
low on the ground
right into that thing
fully consumed
rolling in it.

When I next break the surface
it is as a dolphin
sleek and smooth
calmed and light
jumping the waves
laughing with delight.

And there is a poem.

GREEN

Do you know green?

Tzaneen green?
Transkei green?
Thoyandou green?
Valley of a Thousand Hills green?

It holds me
breathes calm into me
cleanses me
makes me lush

Do you know green?

Forbidden to Dream

CRY

(retrenched man)

Sombawo
have mercy on me.

shivering with sweat
the earth roaring softly past
relentless going away from me,
crushed and angry
not knowing what I have known
that I am a working man,
not doing what I had loved
putting food on the table for my little ones
rent in the moment of sadness
shattered in instant of total possession
all that was real taken away
my pride stripped,
filled with emptiness.

for a little while
I wept sorrowfully
that the normal is not for me anymore
the man, the husband
the head, the provider
u-tata
it would not be me anymore.

I wept for myself
I wept for my wife
I wept for my children,
I wept for my close
And distant extended families,
I wept.

Sombawo,
have mercy on me.

IN THE FIRE

In that cold night
You gathered the wood
To light the rusty brazier
To warm your heart and bodies
And to keep the flames of your togetherness
Breathing life of passion

Love was burning through the darknight
Until you melted and burnt to darkashes
As you were loving each other
In the fire

A WISH

I wanted to take you to dinner
Last night (it was Saturday)
But
My conscience wouldn't let me
After seeing empty stomachs
Around me
So,
With those few cents
I feed them

ANOTHER SHACK

Sitting on and empty paint tin
Warming myself on a brazier in a shack
Balancing my head between my hands
Thinking about the father I never have
Who denied me before I was even born,
Lifting my head up
I saw a young girl with a big belly-pregnant,
With earnest face and wet tearful eyes
Searching for the father
Who disappeared into the township.

I looked into the skies
I see the future bleak for the unborn
The road direct to another shack
Just like this one
Where the child will only think about
The father he never had.

TEARS OF RICHMOND

You say I must sing
Sing of roses
Roses red
Red with blood
Blood by my brothers and sisters
You say I must sing...Ingoapele
Madingoane.

As darkness falls in the quiet hour
Of the day,
Faceless, callous killers creep
And sneak to your huts
While you are asleep
Heavily – armed with their
AK47's and assegais

To fill your bodies with bullets
And cut you into pieces of flesh.

The rolling hills of Kwa-Zulu
Bleed again...

I was watching on tv
Gory evidence of the savagery
With which the massacre
Was carried out

The sadness and cries of your
Beloved ones
With their cold stern faces
Some venting their anger at God
Calling on Him
To prevail
But in vain

They call and call
Until more and more
Died...

Death invades the villages
Of Magoba and Indaleni
The tv news reader

Read on...
While I was trying
To hold back my tears
With quiet anger boiling my soul.

DARK CHILD

I have been told all my life
Again and again
To keep on trying
Until the end
Not to surrender
Even when day becomes night
Even when disappointments mount
To intolerable proportions
I have been told

But when is the end
How do I know when to give up
To throw in the towel

Do I have to go down
To the bowels of the earth
Trying for betterment

Yes, they said
Keep on trying
Dark child
Until you die
It will be all over someday
Trust in God.

FORBIDDEN TO DREAM

(My friend – Ayanda Banzane)

At times
I felt very lonely
Longing for a friend
I have lost in you

In our young photos
I spied some forgotten phases
Of our yesteryears
When we stood in a street corner
Mapping our lives

We were hoping that someday to be some-
body
In this township where dreams have no
meaning at all
How innocently we were inspired
By the guts of Sobukwe and Biko
Who brought a shift of our consciousness

Those were the days
My friend
Before your migration
To greener pastures
Now you live faraway
We share no more of our innermost joys and
sorrows

Time and age has spoiled our lives
Changing the way we were

HATE

Selecting words
To express feelings and seeings
Of how I hate the deceitful fake reconcilia-
tion
That other man lives within and the prejudi-
cial way
He handles my life,
Demoting – taking me down
In every stride I made

How I hate to see a man
Whose beard grew grey
Working in a lane
Craving for positions he will never get
Because his skin colour
Is black like Biko's dream

It is all a conspiracy
A race against another race
Patronizing each other
With pretentious smiles

Really
Black is black
White is white
We are all men in colour.

OUR LOVE
(For my son Khanyiso)

I looked at your face
and I saw my image in your eyes

months ago,
you were the life inside your mother
lodged in her inner space
like a star growing brighter everyday
taking on its own identity
and beauty and form.

You are a creation of our love
not a result of a brief meeting
of flesh without love,

even though we had not planned
to create you
but you were created
out of love

with you in my arms
I could not but think
about my trouble life
which has been clouded by pain,
pain of being fatherless
and pain of being poor,

after watching you asleep
lost in your quite thoughts
I swear to god
no child
I brought into this world
would ever know either of those pains
I swear to god...

THE CELL

When they push me in that cell
Those bars and walls replaced home
Old life blew away
All that was sweet turned sour
Nothing left
But all the time in the world
to spend inside these grey cold hard walls,
scribbled with graffiti
"life is like a weather, my brother watch out".

First night no sleep,
Witnessing all that coldness
And I break down and cry
Oh mama ... I want to come home.

Like a cage bird in my cell
I watch the world pass me by.

AWAKE

(Poem Mzwakhe should have written)

God is on my side
To find a soul that was lost
In a miscarriage of justice
Blessed by others, swearing false oaths
Ravaged by power-lust.

I shall return
Awake like Lazarus...
And cling deep within your soul
Chanting poetic verses
With my robust voice
Like days before
Starting the revolution
Telling the truth – nothing but the truth

THROUGH HUNGER

(To Thandile Kona)

Busy as ever
In the streets of Port Elizabeth in central,
Content with my company of thoughts
Caring less for the passer-by
I stumble to and old man
Garbed in dirty clothes near to a rags
Without looking back
I said, I am sorry
Uncaring

He called me back with a warm smile,
Wondering to myself
What was he going to say,
Politely he mutters:
Don't be sorry, be careful next time son

Strange
That through hunger and cold
He can still speak
Words of wisdom.

DEEP

You age before you grave
That visit so short-lived
Only footprints left in the sands of time.

You withered away
Like autumn trees, blown away
By blazing winds
With a song so deep in message

But time heals all wounds
And pain of deeper ones like yours.

A life so promising
Still expecting so much from you.

EULOGY

Moses came
In a pillar of songs
To show us the way
As a gift from the gods
Lamenting
Calling and calling
Leading us to the One
In search of our genes and spirits

He vented his life on piano
Sliding his long hands to reach
The furthest keys
His face a mask of concentration and wry-
ness
But it did not help him
To hang on to life

Moses left (very passionate, very tormented
man)
In a pillar of silence
To unburden his soul
"finding one self"
conquered.

IN

Themba ka
Mathe

Disturbing the Dead

too long gone

she hugs me,
couples it up with a red kiss
siss!
i feel the chillness of her bloodless breast
and the aridness of her lips
could have been love
fondling poker–dot covered chicken thighs
"are you new?"
all of us probably too old,
for the cops to care.
wasted!
she would never understand my nightmares
or picture my naïve dreams
she has been standing there for a long future,
faking screams
sucking dicks,
just to prop her twisted desires
a town house, bmw, a cell phone and a jackpot machine
just not for now,
in the other life

perhaps tonight
hoping for better pickings
banking on fast-tracked
infernal emotions.
but my mboweni tigers tripled
won't even be enough
to cover for her rent
next month
or her funeral last week.
i stare at her,
racing towards her end

can't stop her
back peddling
she blows
a real kiss this time
but she is gone
too long

wait, give me a chance

let them celebrate mama
this is my day
as when you were born.
wait give me a chance
don't i deserve it.

wait for a moment .... mama
don't deny me my right,
my right - right to action
it is your woman's right
i know
but why deny another woman
her maiden right
how far then can you ejaculate your right?
whose right is right?
stand for our rights mama
human rights
no death rattles.

like a barren tree,
your labour shall bear no fruits
is it not a shame?
hold me in your hands,
swing me down and low,
sweet mama.
for once i will be your daughter, your son,
your child
a gift.
for once i will fill the emptiness of your life
your consolator.

wait and search your soul, mama
should
i
silently and innocent

of a sacrificial lamb depart forever
but seriously, mama, the world needs me
and i too lust after it.
wait mama, think not only of today,
for tomorrow is a day of reckoning.

isn't life a precious gift mama ?
give it to me then,
as a present today, this present day
wait and listen to my cry,
cry of joy - joy to be - so sweet.
listen to my call, composed call
you are within call - i know
the endless call ....
mama this is for you
wait ! mama ! wait !
wait ! mama !
wait !
waa...it!

the bone war

odd,
that dogs and cats
fight
and never win
the bone war.
out of the way,
my hands
are longer,
and get faster
into the garbage bin.
a straggler,
an enemy
wins,
cringe makingly.

the return journey

today we return,
unwillingly,
defeated and humiliated
to you,
 our birth soils
shoved along pot-holed paths
to a life deplorable,
never contemplated:
but tell me,
of what worth shall we be?

from where shall we start ?
tell me - all over again?
after all that pride and honour
for so long a time,
basking and grilling in the hunter's gear
fortune perceived to be dripping
down our attenuate thighs
by our own kind,
from hearsay.

yes the truck is parked
 backwards
today
we return,
back to a part of the native land
never moved with the movement of times
left behind,
but not so graceful.
imagine what we were
and have become,
my beloved;
times do change
and life can be strange.

this day embargoed,
we revert to our roots,
vulnerable to the million prying eyes.
how then will the lost kingdom
remember the long gone sons and daugh-
ters?
tell me about these pilgrimages;
of their health and much talked about
wealth,
precious youth and farewell oaths
perhaps left somewhere
behind

never to be recovered

see us now:
tails coiled between our legs
we take to a down-trodden track
maybe you know.
to the numerous inquisitive questions
nagging us all the way to shame
answers.
answers
in multitude.
bits and pieces
defensive.
Unconvincing.

drink my blood

drink my blood
for i'm still down
and bleeding
the sword is still DEEP
inside,
take it out
so i can get some rest
and you
your conquest medal.

ode to thomas khoza

i see this shadow everyday
so dark,
hounding and sliding
and sliding
it hangs all over our lives,
more-over a journey separates us now,
should i recall your words,
smiles and our travelled miles in verse...tom?
thirty-four chasing thirty-five, with a chance
for more
your golden sun,
rising against probabilities of grumbling
clouds,
just crumbled

gently, fragile and yet firm...
do i remember you well tom?
trying to hold time with your bulky hands,
it never was a forlorn task.
 from the refined brown dunes of warmbat-
hs,
the yellow stone of johannesburg
 never fell in front of you,
you smelt it deeper
 only in the carltoneville mines
where your youth was stolen.
in good times
you lost your heart to jean
she is the only one i saw
yet queens found joy pronouncing your
name...
tom, tom, poppy

your mind, sharp, quick and enquiring
always engaged in the scrabble of beautifully

crafted words
you lost no time in knowing talent
because you had it in your green blood,
taken at no cost,
one more life lost to thugs' bullets
see how they run,
moving in the labyrinth of muddle
no witness,
only passer-bys.

but remember tom...
among us you reside strong
like anywhere else you walked,
leaving footprints,
as always with your ready smiles
even in that demolished face,
silently sleeping there,
in the government mortuary.
just another unidentified body
buried alive.
unknown and naked.

*(in the memory of thomas khoza, a poet, writer, a colleague
and friend who tragically passed away in 2000 at the turbine
hall, newtown johannesburg.)*

his story

scratching the delicate brain-WHITE-
watched head
little boy scholar
takes his weight off the feet
leaning beside a dry mopane tree
overlooking his grandfather's idle kraal
gazing fixedly – at an old dog-eyed text
and twelve futures ahead.

memorizing word by word,
the contents
of his country's twisted history.
plugging his eyes for a while
to spread out his delicate mind
to the worst of his maze
though he tries best.

nonetheless,
was not clear to him
how it all started,
happened and possible ended.
even her mother
could not convince him,
of his dad's non-existence.

probably died.
but how, why and where exactly?
may be in the british war
boer war, french war or dutch war
how could that have been?
would he merely go and fight in europe
for what worthy cause?

surely it confuses him.
the demeanour,

grandpa relates sad tales of his
huge stock of cattle perished in and gone
with the advent of great wars
and how pathetic it does not coincide
with HIS recorded STORY.

though, his teacher pushes him on
to read and pass
now he was two minded,
of sea waves
refusing to be still
hurrying to the sea-shore
and back to its core.

line after line
his story became art
and was without a clue
how one person,
too WHILD for that matter
discovered a large piece
of black populated land.

but why,
in this brief being
worry, about such trivial issues?
after all, it matters to know
about one's history
above all, it mattered most
where he got his story from.

a moving machine

you !
is that you
who has changed?
red, yellow, green
so sudden
like a chameleon
again.
yet,
you
don't even know
of the make over
or it's another work
of the programmer
and you are
still
the same,
like others -
a moving robot.

tich mataz

tich mataz is no longer
running these shores
he walked the streets,
left-foot first,
in a razz mataz fashion
dead trembling in fear

the police officer came
straight to him at once
fast and rough as a tiger,
in the kruger national
suck out operation
jaw-clapping on his black figure-belt

questions later,
his papers were not in western order
a bite on the back
he could not speak for them.
in his gawky and jagged tongue
from afrika.

the quick pushes to the van
left him chilling cold
he spent his dreams at lindela
and abandoned all
his african renaissance hopes
across the boarder post.

pushing away

again
it's hitting hard on my nose
trying to push away the truth
forgetting is not easy
hit the holy weed,
and down the brown bottle
wear the face of triumph
not yet!

too deceiving

internal conflict

never tell them, we live side by side
comb my remains
 i am not where you see me.
from my mental territory,
i have shifted
into another world
we are no longer together now.
                        confront my mental
institution.
for i am fighting complex wars here
though strong armies i have assembled,
the simmering conflict is severe
against my own kind
snarled knives slay me off your world.
the more i move closer,
wider apart i drift
looking from above this mountain
down the gorge,
 i see you
pretentious
as to visualise a soul up there
strengthen your scrutiny,
i am so far away
lest you delude your vision,
i am too many people
wrapped
in one heavy blanket
refusing to give me a night's sleep.
i have departed beyond your understanding
never mind
or ever tell them, we live side by side
i too, am struggling to find myself
i am too far away.

days

duplicated hours
unreel and blonk hallowly
days, abysmally conceived.

is there any visible essence?
when ours are marked –
deep scarlet

and already numbered:
pettishly in these virile
street-couchettes of johannesburg.

fallen woman

from very far, i saw them
in their high-heeled shoes
hip-high slit skirts
and mini skirts
appearing and disappearing
in the simmering clouds
of their bountiful pastel spell.

they lined up
against the graffitied concrete walls
parading their wares on the side walks
bravely, exhibiting without shame
to reach as far as marketable,
their intimate endowments.

in all shapes and sizes
tons of jewellery dangle and tangle
down powdered necks and wrists.
vipers' rims oppressively smeared
for judas' kisses
to preach,
they substituted the priest
in religions of death and repugnance.

they came all the way
with love to spread it to all.
but who could afford
a small service fee.
the kiss and tell randy-andys
in posh cars one after the other
slow down to negotiate
"a quick round or an all night joy ride"
which ever quenches their temporary craving
and zoom away into twilight's darkness.

trucks in long processions
deserting home-brewed love
to pick and choose on the street menu
weighing up the strength of each other,
down to the bottom of their wallets
oblivious of the corrode speed
of the century's capricious virus
teeth sharpened for another vulnerable statis-
tic
entirely indiscriminate of their class and
cause,
misguided beliefs and deep-rooted myths.

still the gypsy girl stands
lingering by the street corner
waiting for a call.
beautiful,
as art
art..ificially from the skin to the teeth
insatiable in their canal knowledge,
wringing and twisting
her wasted waist.
to where?
until when?
ladies of charm,
forget your bottom power:
yours has matured beyond frolic.
the writing is patent
and dripping
deep scarlet on the wall
no matter how tall you stand.

whose truth?

truth the light
that sets humanity free
is tinted
in multiple colours
and you too
have your own truth
not written in
your face.

i'm still thinking

i'm still thinking
perhaps too much
yes, in my think tank
lines of thought are racing,

to and fro
colliding with one another
forming ideas, reviving lost memories
synthesising imaginations - strange ones
indeed.

down in my mind
thoughts and images play – a chasing game
hide and seek
in all directions.

they meet, blend and converge
to make way for dreams
a whole lot of responsibilities follow
while i'm still thinking

and now i'm duty-bound
to perform and deliver
but serious, where do i start
i'm still thinking

IN

Righteous the
Common Man

The Seed of Life

THEY HAVE LANDED

The landless have landed
Where
The landless have landed
Where
The landless have landed
Where

In the land of the landlessness
except for those who have stacks
of cash in their pockets
the rest of the masses remain condemned
shifted from pavements to shacks
battling to escape concentration camps
Where hunger and power struggles
create mad conditions of living
but the landless have landed
to reclaim their stolen wealth

The landless have landed where
The landless have landed
Where? The landless have landed
Where? The landless have landed

In the land of the landlessness
Golden hand shakes have taken place
resulting in misrepresentation undertaken
by false preachers and foolish leaders
No trespassing signs placed
in every gateway
But my investigation's still underway
Operation crack down
Stolen treasures lost and found
in the hands of a few wicked men
enslaved by greed

bearurocratic instruments
who suppress the voices of the masses
replacing land redistribution with a silly mar-
ket system
a confusing solution
that excludes the dispossessed
and promotes the oppression
of the cashless

But the landless have landed
Where
The landless have landed
Where
The landless have landed

In the landless planet
The land of landlessness
Escaping from shacks
And concentration camps
To reclaim the stolen wealth
The landless have landed

BRING BACK THE TIME

Bring back the time

When innocence was still in style
That was the time when sucking milk from your mother's breast
was the only best way to satisfy your appetite
Bring back the time when your unselfishness
and sense of self were still intact
That was when love, joy and trust were
the only inhabitants of your heart
that made you understand the needs of your fellow man
That was the time before seeds of jealousy and greed
were planted in your fragile innocent mind
When everything seemed plain, simple and beautiful
because hatred had not entered your heart

Bring back the time

When your spirit of charity
had not been killed by vanity
That was the time when the status or colour
of others did not matter
When sharing a smile with a stranger
was a given possibility
The time when your innocent curiosity was protected by honesty
That was when integrity was the main ingredient
in mankind's survival recipe
That was the time when love and affection were still in fashion
because they were not yet replaced by exploitation
That was when dehumanisation couldn't be mistaken for civilization
Bring back the time when love was the only thing you had to know
and the only thing you'd show everyone you'd come to know

Bring back the time when love ruled the universe

TOO MANY STRUGGLES

Too many struggles
Messing up my mental muscles
Many stumble in bundles
As they fumble to juggle shores
Always moving back and forth
Like waves do at sea shores
Inflicting multiple septic sores
In the hearts of the poor

Too many struggles, no common direction
To lead us on the path of reconstruction
While others struggle for reconstruction
Many hustle for recognition
Competition rapidly replacing co-operation

Too many struggles
slowing down the pace
silencing major voices of pain
who are crying out loud
for meaningful change

Too many struggles
too many fights too many quarrels
will we ever have one struggle
for economic and social justice
coz too many struggles

will suppress our precious muscles
the masses

MY REALITY

Excuse me, I didn't mean to be
rudely intruding with confusion
it's just that you see it is so amusing
the way you have a tendency of assuming
whenever you speak of solutions and revolutions
concluding that we all share the same reality

Well the truth is
if we don't, we'll fail to change the situation
and this exercise is really time consuming
it is no delusion
that these walls which seem to be closing in
are covered in misery, creating my reality
which is never seen of TV?

I am not talking 'bout your reality
coz yours is always embracing TV screens
your reality's always covering glossy magazines
your reality created by varsities
of CNN, SABC and DSTV's pop videos
and by all of those who control the flow of info

As IMF, World Bank and WTO control the cash flow
my reality is forcibly and continuously confronting poverty
my reality is never seen at cocktail parties
you see my reality never meets with sausages, wine and cheese
coz my reality often sleeps where there's nothing to eat
The music that my reality dances to is created by screams
and grooves of gunshots, bullet wounds decorate walls of my reality
blood-dripping bullet wounds decorate walls of my reality
blood-dripping bullet wounds decorate walls of my reality

Angry faces of frustration is always greet
frozen tears I cry, Children with hungry faces I see
no tears in their eyes, all I see are stains
as alcoholism, prostitution and criminalism create pathways
for those who seek to escape from this reality cage
My reality hardly ever meets yours on TV
coz my reality can hardly afford to pay electricity
she lives in the dark, far away from economic activities
If you've ever seen my reality before, it probably means
you and me must be related, and your reality might be
my reality, together we can then start thinking
about changing that reality, and that's MY REALITY
not a talk about revolution!

A COMMON MAN

The sun shines so bright to bring the true essence of life to all
mankind
Light, warmth and love are all provided to us by the sun
But only a few of us can recognise the beauty that is shown to
us by the sunlight
Some can't even feel the warmth that is provided to us by the
sun, why?
It is because they can't feel the heat like Robert De Niro?
Since their bodies are cold because their souls' temperatures
are way below Zero
Degrees, they cease to live but continue to exist
Cruising without a compass in this ship of life
Their direction is guided by what they can see only through
their two eyes
Minds are paralysed, they are intoxicated
high and hypnotized by what their eyes make them see
They can't feel anything, think or even blink
as their life ship sinks deep under the blood sea
Drowning in their own blood with no hope
of a lifeboat or even self-pride to hold on to
But who am I to tell you what I see through these three eyes
of mine?
I am just a common man
A common man trying to make some sense out of this mys-
tery of life
I'm a common man guided by two of my best friends
Common sense and the one within myself,
The immortal Warrior

I'm not perfect, I'm just a common man who's not even edu-
cated
Maybe if I was, I'd get their attention
Or maybe if I was rich and famous, I bet I'd still get their
attention
But I have no education and neither do I have earthly riches

All I am enriched with is the inspiration to give you this information

That's provided to me by the one within

I'm passing it on to you hoping you will make use of it

In an attempt to avoid the truth, fools would try to mute my voice

I watch them fail as my words continue striking you like lightning

Striking a tree

I got you open, sending chills down your spine

Foolish smiles turn into frowns

As suckers realize that I can't be shut down

Coz I'm this common man protected by the most high power

To the creator of nature, I am one of the most beautiful flowers

In this already messed up garden

Planet called earth

To you I will always be a common man

A common man trying to make some sense of this mystery of life

I am a common man trying to put together the puzzles of the picture of life

I hope my words will make some sense to you

If they don't now, then they will some day

I hope when the day comes, it won't be too late

You don't have to know my name, but just who I am

And who I am is a common man

Far from perfect, but quite close to righteousness.

REMEMBER ME

Remember me the common man
from the land of the common people
where poverty pierces souls of the feeble
like needles do skins of dizzy junkies

Remember me when you see
that hungry kid begging for money
to buy poisonous sweets,
before he goes to sleep
in a filthy corner of the streets

Remember me coz you see
that's my brother,
a product of a runaway father
your brother's keeper's cousin
who was never there to raise him

He was raised by harsh streets
that taught him how to be mean brave
he never saw love, all knows is how to hate
watch out as he allows his rage to escape
your wife, mother and daughter are about to get raped

Remember me when that happens
and ask yourself if you've planted
enough seeds of love for you
to seek peace in this wicked land

Remember me coz you see
everything you are about to see
is just another repetition
of the future's history

Remember me when you see

that small red dot between
the lifeless eyes of your beloved brother
ask yourself if this evil action
of your fellowman's off-spring
is a true reflection of your own contribution
to the human population

Remember me when you are in your lovely car
waiting for that red light to turn green
then suddenly through your windscreen
you see a man-made compassionless sub-human being
pointing a deadly instrument to your head
Your heart stops to beat
you find it hard to breathe
your cell phone is hard to reach
you cannot call the police
on a number that's toll free 0800 11 12 13

Remember me when that happens
and ask yourself if these evil deeds
of your fellowman's off-spring
are true returns of your teachings to society

Remember me when these casualties of reality
are suffered by the ones you love and need
ask yourself if you and your fellowman
have planted enough seeds of love
for you to seek peace in this wicked land

Remember me the common man
from the land of common people
where poverty pierces souls of the feeble
like needles do skins of dizzy crack junkies

this is where mental malnutrition
turns kids into super-killing machines
trigger happy creatures who never hesitate to kill
sucking all your blood until you stop to bleed

Remember me when you realize the need
for you and me to INCREASE love and peace
before these cannibals of reality
swallow all those we love and need

Remember me, INCREASE LOVE PEACE!

REMEMBERING THE TIMES

Like a real soldier
You carried fierce battles on your shoulders
Walking side by side
You and me on straight line
Fighting wickedness, from the same side
Many battles have been won
But the struggles continues to go on

I still vividly remember
Those times when we lived like brothas
Breaking bread together
You on the forefront, like a father
A reliable bread provider
Making sure that we neva gave up

I remember those times
Which are now long gone
From a distance I see you taking strolls
With those who oppressed us before
You no longer respond
To my desperate calls
Except of course
When you need me at the polls

JUST BECAUSE

Just because you put an x
To select your trusted government
Thus that make you a free man?
Even though you only have in your hands
Less than thirteen percent of the land
While the rest is being controlled by the white man

Just because you are black
Does that make you an African?
Expecting me to call you my brother
Just because we share the same skin colour
But when the hunger thunder strikes
You stand on the opposite side
Of the dividing poverty line

Just because you read about the loxion
Does it mean you know the culture
Coz ma brotha, is still live in it
Just because you speak of a revolution
Does it mean you have all the solutions
For the confusion I might be going through

Just because you sit with them
Discussing issues on round tables
Does it mean you can't be fooled by their fables?
Just because they gave you crumbs
Now you feel that you own the cake
And you fight to celebrate
Pick up the pace and finish the race
Coz in the game of the economatrix
You are nothing but a bar-coded faceless name
This game's dominated by monsters
All that you are is just a porn star

Just because you hear of a renaissance
You think is the end of resistance
But you still suffocating from foreign expert assistance
Just because BANTU education has left
Does it mean BIKO's consciousness
Must be put to rest
Without consciousness
How will you make a positive stand?

Just because you walk in the same streets
With your former enemies
You believe there's enough peace and harmony
Although millions are still living in poverty
Just because we are having the TRC
Continuously granting amnesty
Does that guarantee justice
And economic equality

Wake up from fancy dreams
And smell the burning trees
Smell the burning trees
Smell the burning trees

IN SEARCH OF FREEDOM

So many clear visions, perfect pictures
So many decisions
beautiful thoughts captured
in eternal motions
So many words of wisdom being spoken
yet remain frozen
Trapped in cages of ignorance
Bloated minds impregnated with arrogance

So many books written, from dark ages
Scriptures scattered in burned pages
Buried deep underneath
Shallow graves of vanity

While choosing to walk only with the dead
We fail to read these unedited scrolls
The oppressed feeble souls
Try to sing songs of freedom
Their songs get blocked
By the wicked hand of king kong
The one masquerading as man-god
Playing ping-pong with human souls
In a favourite game show of cyber folks
I'm sorry I meant to say human clones

So many revelations, educations and civilizations
So much space for the elevation of mind body and spirit
To complete the ultimate mission
So much so many so many so much
Yet so little being done to protect humanity

So many thick volumes of doctrines
Filled with religious and isms
And many other man-made divisions
So many prophecies and philosophies

So many histories
Documentation of people's miseries
So many promises made in these
Oppressive economic policies
Yet little is being done to protect
the oppressed societies

so many years of living
In pain, fear and throwing stones
16 June, 76 was the year
When we got choked by tear gas smoke
Beyond 2G we still search for gun free zones
As we are getting killed for these cell phones
So much pain, so many eroding gains
But the question remains
SO WHERE TO?

So many deaths and wars
So many summits and world class talk shops
So many talks about walking the talk
It's funny how you're still talking
And not walking
Shit man! Could this be the end of the
beginning
or the beginning of the end
as I stop the talking and
continue with my walking
in search of freedom

NOTES ABOUT CONTRIBUTORS

NOSIPHO KOTA was born in 1974, in New Brighton, Port Elizabeth. Her interest in writing was sparked by her love for words and books. She started writing poetry when she was studying at King William's Town in the early 1980s. She wrote in Xhosa and kept the manuscript hidden. She did not believe that she was a writer let alone a poet. In 1991, at a ten-day vacation school at the University of Port Elizabeth, her love for writing was once again validated by a newspaper that she compiled for the group. From then on, friends and family members kept on nudging her to do something about her writing. Her first break came in the form of a month that she spent at a daily newspaper then called The Evening Post. She also freelanced for several publications and did not stop writing poetry. Her poetry has been published in several anthologies and journals, including Writing From Here, New Coin, New Contrast, Kotaz, Timbila and Fidelities. She now works for East Cape Weekend, a Saturday newspaper in Port Elizabeth. In 2001 and 2002, she was awarded the East Cape Vodacom's Journalist of the Year Award.

ALEX MBOSHWA MOHLABENG, born and grew up in Seshego township near Polokwane in Limpopo started writing poetry during his first year at Setotolwane College of Education where he obtained a Teacher's Diploma in 1994. Currently a teacher, a few of his poems have been published in two volumes of a creative writing journal, Turfwrite, founded and edited by Prof. John Ruganda of the University of the North and in Timbila.

MYESHA JENKINS is an African-American who relocated to South Africa after writing her first poem here, in 1991. "I am grateful to this land for giving me my creativity". She is passionate about gender equality, jazz, spirit. Her writing has been published in Timbila, Botsotso and True Love. She can be found in jazz clubs, bookstores and friends' k'tchens in and around Johannesburg.

AYANDA BILLIE was born on February 17, 1975, in the dusty township of Kwa-Nobuhle, Uitenhage in the Eastern Cape. He grew up in a matchbox 4-roomed house under the care of his grandmother Madabane intombi yase Maqocweni. At the age of 11 he started developing an interest in books. He passed his matric at Phaphani High School. He is a member of Ucwadi Writers Association in PE-Uitenhage. He writes poetry, short stories, newspaper and magazine articles.

THEMBA KA MATHE born 1973, describes himself as a poet first and foremost, as well as a writer, journalist and human rights activist. He has shared the stage with both Linton Kwesi Johnson and Mutabaruka. His articles, book reviews and general profiles have appeared in newspapers such as City Press, Sowetan Sunday World,

Mail & Guardian, Sunday Independent, the Sowetan, New Africans, Homeless Talk, and several other newspapers. His poems have appeared in Timbila 2002, Global Fire, NGO Matters and Of Money Mandarins and Peasants. Themba lives in Yeoville, Johannesburg.

RIGHTEOUS THE COMMON MAN was born in Meadowlands, Gauteng. He has performed his poetry during the World Conference Against Racism, Xenophobia & Related Intolerance in Durban, Jubilee South Africa activities, SANGOCO NGO Week in Durban, Movement for Delivery workshop at Zava in Giyani and in other meetings where issues of social justice are discussed. Portions of Word-the seed of life which is his unpublished poetry collection have been published in Timbila, Community Gazette, Global Fire, Izwi labantu, Anti-Privatisation Forum Monitor, NGO Matters, SAGDA News among other publications. Currently, Righteous the Common Man is working on his poetry and music CD.

ALAN FINLAY has published two collections of poems: "Burning Aloes" (Dye Hard Press, 1994) and "riverrain" (included in No Free Sleeping, Botsotso Publishing, 1998). His poems have appeared in numerous local journals. He co-edited Parking Space: A collection of Eastern Cape High School Poetry with Robert Berold (ISEA, 1994) and has taught poetry to learners in Alexander, Gauteng. Besides organisizing poetry readings at the Grahamstown National Arts Festival, he edited and published the literary journal Bleksem (1994-1997) and currently edits and publishes the online literary journal, Donga (www.donga.co.za). He works in the field of ICT development in the non-profit sector.

SIPHIWE KA NGWENYA was born at Phiri in the early sixties and now lives at Dlamini 2, Soweto. He is a poet, dramatist, translator and editor. He has published poetry in publications such as Ingolovane, Buang Basadi, Mother Tongues, Timbila, New Coin, Botsotso, Tribute, Essential Things, We Jive Like This and Dirty Washing. He has performed poetry and participated in literary activities in Southern Africa, Sweden, Denmark, Canada and Pakistan. He is a member of Jozi Book Club and Botsotso Jesters, a group of performance poets in Johannesburg.